AMERICA GOES TO WAR

THE VIETNAM WAR

TIMELINES, FACTS, AND BATTLES

I0814204

By Craig Boutland

Published in 2023 by The Rosen Publishing Group, Inc.
2544 Clinton Street, Buffalo, NY 14224

Copyright © 2022 Brown Bear Books Ltd.

All rights reserved. No part of this book may be reproduced in any form without permission in writing from the publisher, except by a reviewer.

Editor: Lindsey Lowe
Children's Publisher: Anne O'Daly
Design Manager: Keith Davis
Picture Manager: Sophie Mortimer

Picture Credits:
Front Cover: Public Domain
Key: t = top, b = bottom, c = center
Alamy: Everett Collection Historical 40b, PJF Military Collection 40t; Library of Congress: 40-41, 46c; Pubic Domain: 16t, AFP/Stringer 16-17b, Johannes Barre, iGEL 10-11b, Michael Darter 61b, Forteplan/Nagy Gyula 10-11t, Musee ANNM 17t, Store norske leksikon 61c, The Peoples Republic of China Printing Office, 10b, 11t, Vietnam People's Army Museum 16-17t; Robert Hunt Library: 6, 7, 8, 9, 13, 14, 30, 39, 45, 49, 51t, 58, 59t, 59b; United States Government: 16b, Department of Defense 28b, U.S. Army 22b, 23t, 28t, 29, 34, 35c, 35t, Information Agency 28-29, U.S. Marines 60-61, 61t, U.S. Navy 60t, USAF 22t; U.S. National Archives: 5, 12,15, 18, 19, 20, 21, 22-23b, 24, 25, 26t, 26b, 27, 32, 33t, 33b, 34-35, 36, 38t, 38b, 41t, 42, 43, 44, 46t, 46-47, 47, 48, 50, 51b, 52, 54, 55, 56, 57.

Cataloging-in-Publication Data

Names: Boutland, Craig.
Title: The Vietnam War: timelines, facts, and battles / Craig Boutland.
Description: New York : Rosen Publishing, 2023. | Series: America goes to war| Includes bibliographic references, index and glossary.
Identifiers: ISBN 9781499473889 (pbk) | ISBN 9781499473896 (library bound) | ISBN 9781499473902 (ebook)
Subjects: LCSH: Vietnam War, 1961-1975— Juvenile literature
Classification: LCC DS557.7 B68 2023 | DDC 959.704/3—dc23

Manufactured in the United States of America

CPSIA Compliance Information: Batch #CWRYA23. For further information contact Rosen Publishing at 1-800-237-9932.

Find us on 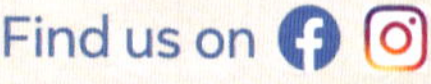

CONTENTS

Introduction

The Vietnam War was already underway when the United States become actively involved in 1963; it lasted another 12 years and cost 50,000 U.S. lives.

An independence campaign led by the Viet Minh had split the French colony of Vietnam into two countries in 1946: communist North Vietnam, backed by China and the Soviet Union, and the French-sponsored Republic of Vietnam.

The Course of the War

The reason the war was not simply a local conflict lay in the strategic struggles of the Cold War. U.S. politicians feared the spread of Soviet communism. The so-called domino theory suggested that if one country in a region became communist, others would follow. When North Vietnamese military action forced a French withdrawal from Vietnam, therefore, the Americans chose to step in. They began by sending advisors to help the Army of the Republic of Vietnam (ARVN), but their military presence quickly grew as fighting broke out. The main clashes came near the demilitarized zone (DMZ), or "no-man's land." There was also extensive guerrilla warfare in the South, conducted by the Viet Cong, an underground army. Facing a determined enemy, rising casualty figures, and increasing protests at home, the United States transferred responsibility for fighting to its South Vietnamese allies and had withdrawn its troops before the final fall of the South in April 1975.

About This Book

This book contains two types of timelines. Along the bottom of the pages is a timeline that covers the whole period. It lists key events and developments, color coded to indicate events in the land and air campaigns or in the political field. Each chapter also has its own timeline, which runs vertically down the sides of the pages. This timeline gives more specific details about the particular subject of the chapter. IN FOCUS spreads give more information on key events, personalities, and weapons.

Soldiers of the 4th Infantry Division take cover at the edge of a field during an operation in October 1967.

Causes of the War

What began as an attempt to shore up a friendly regime in South Vietnam escalated from 1965 into a military test of will for the United States and the most divisive issue of the age.

➔ Viet Minh independence fighters take possession of Haiphong in 1955 after the withdrawal of the French.

TIMELINE **1950–1963**

KEY: Air War | Land War | Politics

1950 | 1955

March 20, 1954 United States
U.S. leaders discuss helping the French in Indochina, where French forces are besieged at Dien Bien Phu.

May 7, 1954 North Vietnam
Dien Bien Phu falls to the Viet Minh, Vietnamese independence fighters.

January 1, 1955 South Vietnam
The first U.S. military advisors arrive in South Vietnam to help the new republic.

January 1958 South Vietnam
North Vietnam decides to launch a takeover of South Vietnam.

Vietnam in Southeast Asia occupies part of the Southeast Asian peninsula formerly known as Indochina, which also includes Thailand, Myanmar (Burma), Laos, and Cambodia.

The Europeans Arrive

The first Europeans to arrive in Indochina were French Catholic priests in the 17th century. By the 19th century, local rulers wanted to get rid of them and their influence on local people. But the French government protected the priests and sent warships to the area to threaten the local rulers. In 1862, Emperor Tu Duc of Vietnam was forced to sign a treaty with France that protected the priests and gave France the right to trade in the area.

French Take Over

Over the next 20 years, the French sent more people to the region. Indochina was rich in gold, silver, spices, and other precious goods, which the French wanted to control. By 1887,

KEY DATES

March 6, 1946 Ho Chi Minh signs an agreement with the French that recognizes him as president of the Democratic Republic of Vietnam (later called North Vietnam). The French set up a separate state in the South.

December 19, 1946 War breaks out between the French and North Vietnam.

March 20, 1954 American leaders discuss helping the French in Indochina. French forces are surrounded at Dien Bien Phu.

May 7, 1954 Dien Bien Phu falls to the Viet Minh. The French have lost 35,000 men in the war and are forced to leave Vietnam.

January 1, 1955 U.S. military advisors arrive in South Vietnam.

Continued on page 9

John F. Kennedy escalated U.S. involvement in South Vietnam.

1960

August 2, 1961 United States President John F. Kennedy commits the United States to supporting South Vietnam.

January 2, 1963 South Vietnam ARVN (South Vietnamese) soldiers, supplied by the United States, suffer defeat at Ap Bac.

November 22, 1963 United States President Kennedy is assassinated in Dallas.

November 24, 1963 United States New president Lyndon B. Johnson vows to continue U.S. support for South Vietnam.

Dien Bien Phu

The turning point in the war between North Vietnam and the French was the siege of Dien Bien Phu. The French set up a base there in late 1953, behind enemy lines in North Vietnam. The North Vietnamese surrounded it in March 1954 and began a siege. The French were unable to get supplies into the stronghold, and on May 7, they surrendered. Some 2,200 of their 16,000 troops died in the siege.

➔ France ruled Indochina in the 19th century.

they ruled most of Indochina and had decided to incorporate the peninsula into their empire. By the end of the century, around 50,000 French people lived there. Local people were treated as second-class citizens and were very poor. They rose up against the French, but their rebellions were crushed.

Ho Chi Minh

Japan conquered Indochina during World War II but was forced to leave after its defeat in 1945. Communists in Vietnam, led by Ho Chi Minh, seized

➔ French troops watch reinforcements parachute into Dien Bien Phu.

TIMELINE **1964 FEBRUARY–NOVEMBER**

KEY: Air War | Land War | Politics

February | April | August

February 7 South Vietnam
A Viet Cong bomb explodes in a Saigon theater, killing three Americans and wounding 50.

April 25 South Vietnam
General Westmoreland takes charge of Military Assistance Command in Vietnam (MACV).

August 2 Gulf of Tonkin
North Vietnamese torpedo boats attack USS *Maddox* in the Gulf of Tonkin; President Johnson warns that the United States will defend itself.

power. Ho declared himself president in August 1945. In October, French troops arrived to reclaim the country. They captured the South, but in March 1946, the French recognized Ho Chi Minh as president of a new communist country in the North: the Democratic Republic of Vietnam. The French created a new country in the South, later known as the Republic of Vietnam. War broke out in December 1946 as the two sides fought for control of the whole country. The French lost and withdrew, but by then the South Vietnamese had a new supporter: the United States.

The United States

U.S. politicians were concerned that the loss of one country to communism would create a "domino effect" in which neighboring states would also fall to communism.

On August 2, 1961, President John F. Kennedy announced that the United States would do all it could to support South Vietnam and save it from communist takeover. He sent in more military personnel, initially to act as advisors.

Ho Chi Minh led the North Vietnamese war effort.

Continued from page 7

January 1958 North Vietnam begins a campaign to conquer South Vietnam. It orders communist guerrillas operating in South Vietnam to begin the attack.

December 1960 North Vietnam forms the Viet Cong (Vietnamese communists) to fight in South Vietnam.

August 2, 1961 President Kennedy announces that the United States will help South Vietnam.

February 7, 1962 There are now 4,000 U.S. military personnel in South Vietnam, training the South's soldiers.

May 16, 1962 President Kennedy announces that troops will be sent to protect the neighboring country, Thailand.

August 5 North Vietnam U.S. aircraft bomb North Vietnam in retaliation for the attack in the Gulf of Tonkin.

August 5 United States Congress approves the Southeast Asia Resolution, allowing all steps to be taken to protect U.S. personnel within Vietnam.

October

October South Vietnam Some 1,300 U.S. special forces, the Green Berets, arrive in the country.

November South Vietnam A North Vietnamese attack wins control of much of Binh Dinh province in South Vietnam.

November 3 United States Lyndon B. Johnson is elected as president of the United States.

The Cold War

By the end of the 1940s, communism and democracy were locked in a standoff.

The involvement of the United States in Vietnam was an attempt to stop the spread of international communism. Communism was a belief that the resources of a society were best controlled by the state, and that people's freedom to own property and to politically organize was severely limited. The Soviet Union had been the only communist state before World War II. In the late 1940s, however, communism spread to other countries. The countries of eastern and central Europe were occupied by the Red Army and became communist. In East Asia, Soviet forces in North Korea helped a communist government establish itself there. Most important in Asia, a communist regime under Mao Zedong was set up in China in 1949 after a civil war.

Colonialism and Nationalism

The conflict between communism and western democracy became known as the Cold War. Both sides were armed with nuclear weapons and there was a tense standoff for decades. The problem for communist states was that people with a choice would normally choose freedom. Soviet troops crushed attempts by rebellious Hungarians to create a more free society in 1956, for example.

The problem for America was that much of the world was ruled by European colonial powers. Freedom from oppressive colonial rule was what these people wanted, and communist powers helped fight against colonialism. In Asia, the USA feared that communism would spread from China to Vietnam and Southeast Asia. It was this tangle of interests and motives that led to the United States becoming embroiled in the Vietnam War.

KEY DATES

1945 The Red Army is in control of eastern and central Europe and in Asia has pushed as far as the Korean peninsula.

June 1948-May 1949 First big standoff of the Cold War. U.S. transport planes keep Berlin supplied after Stalin cuts land links to the German city, which is surrounded by communist East German territory.

1950-1953 Korean War. U.S. combat forces take on the North Korean and Red Chinese armies after North Korea invades South Korea.

May 1955 Bandung Conference. Many nations newly independent of European colonial control, such as Indonesia and Egypt, agree to find a common course of nonalignment to either the West or to the communist bloc.

February 16, 1959 Revolution in Cuba brings the communist Fidel Castro to power.

October-November 1962 Cuban missile crisis. The United States and the Soviet Union almost go to war over the placement of Russian missiles on Cuba.

1 Immobilized Soviet self-propelled guns on the streets of Budapest, Hungary, as the Red Army tries to put down a pro-democracy rebellion.

2 Mao Zedong, communist ruler of China. U.S. officials saw China as the spearhead of communism in Asia.

3 Communist rulers (from left to right): Nikita Khrushchev of Russia, Mao Zedong of China, Ho Chi Minh of Vietnam, and Soong Ching-ling (Vice President of the People's Republic of China from 1959 to 1975).

4 A symbol of Cold War standoff: barbed wire and lookout posts mark the demilitarized zone between North Korea and South Korea.

The War Escalates

As the political situation in South Vietnam worsened, it became clear that the United States' involvement would have to increase and more troops would be required.

Three Viet Cong fighters stand on top of a captured ARVN M113 armored personnel carrier.

TIMELINE 1965 FEBRUARY–DECEMBER

KEY: Air War | Land War | Politics

February

February 13 North Vietnam
The Americans begin Operation Rolling Thunder, a program of air strikes against targets in North Vietnam.

March 6 South Vietnam
The first large units of U.S. ground troops arrive in South Vietnam.

April

April 7 United States
President Johnson offers North Vietnam an aid program in return for stopping the war; North Vietnam rejects the proposal.

The political situation inside South Vietnam was deteriorating. President Ngo Dinh Diem faced both a liberation campaign waged by Viet Cong (VC) communist guerrillas and growing dissatisfaction from the Buddhists who made up the bulk of the population. The South Vietnamese army (with American approval) launched a coup d'état (revolt) against the president and his brother, both of whom were killed in the first week of November 1963.

U.S. Troops Arrive

Despite political instability in the South, the growing strength of the North and the inauguration of Lyndon B. Johnson as the new U.S. president saw the United States increase its military support to South Vietnam. By the end of 1964, the United States Military Assistance Command, Vietnam (MACV), under General William C. Westmoreland, had grown to more than 20,000 men.

In 1964, the U.S. Marines contingent in Vietnam numbered more than 800 men. The majority were located in South Vietnam's I Corps Tactical Zone (ICTZ), closest to the so-called demilitarized zone

KEY DATES

January 2, 1963 ARVN soldiers, equipped by the United States, suffer a humiliating defeat at the hands of the Viet Cong at Ap Bac.

July 17, 1963 South Vietnamese police put down a protest by 1,000 Buddhists.

November 1, 1963 Military coup in South Vietnam; President Diem is shot dead the next day.

August 2, 1964 North Vietnamese torpedo boats attack the USS *Maddox* in the Gulf of Tonkin.

August 5, 1964 U.S. aircraft bomb North Vietnam in retaliation for *Maddox* attack.

November 1964 Viet Cong and NVA regiments take control of most of Binh Dinh province in South Vietnam; ARVN forces are destroyed or pushed back.

Continued on page 15

This Viet Cong recruit wears typical clothing and carries a mortar stand.

September 18 South Vietnam U.S. aircraft attack Viet Cong positions.

October 14 United States The U.S. Defense Department orders a military draft call for 45,224 men.

November 4 South Vietnam The Battle of the Ia Drang Valley sees heavy losses for both sides.

November 27 South Vietnam The South Vietnamese army suffers a major defeat in battle at the Michelin Rubber Plantation.

December 15 North Vietnam The U.S. Air Force bombs and destroys a North Vietnamese power plant, the first raid on a major industrial target.

October

December

Gulf of Tonkin Incident

On August 2, about 28 miles (45 km) off the North Vietnamese coast in the Gulf of Tonkin, the destroyer USS *Maddox* was attacked by three North Vietnamese gunboats. One was disabled and a second retreated; the third sprayed the *Maddox* with machine-gun fire. On August 4, the *Maddox* and USS *C. Turner Joy* were attacked again by North Vietnamese gunboats. The U.S. ships opened fire, sinking one, and possibly two, North Vietnamese vessels.

(DMZ), a narrow strip of no-man's land separating North and South Vietnam. After a clash in the Gulf of Tonkin in August 1964, the United States became drawn into ground fighting, and President Johnson ordered air strikes against targets in North Vietnam in Operation Rolling Thunder. After South Vietnamese army units suffered a series of defeats on the ground, the U.S. Joint Chiefs of Staff approved sending more U.S. Marines to South Vietnam.

Full-Scale War

By the end of 1965, the war in Vietnam had become an American war. More than 148,300 combat and support troops had been sent to

→ U.S. air power became crucial to the support of ground units.

TIMELINE 1966 JANUARY–NOVEMBER

KEY: Air War | Land War | Politics

January — April — July

January 4 South Vietnam
The Viet Cong use Soviet 120-mm mortars, the heaviest weapon used by them so far, at Khe Sanh.

April 24 South Vietnam
The first major Allied move into enemy territory since 1962 discovers quantities of supplies close to Cambodian border.

July 7–August 2 South Vietnam
Operation Hastings is the largest military action to date by U.S. troops.

South Vietnam. Their allies, the Army of the Republic of Vietnam (ARVN), had 500,000 men in 1965, rising to one million in the 1970s, but many of its officers were corrupt and poorly motivated. In contrast, the 400,000 troops of the North Vietnamese Army (NVA) were well trained, well led, and had high morale.

Inside South Vietnam, the VC were at least 10,000 strong in 1965. Nicknamed "Charlie" by the Americans, most VC guerrillas were recruited in the South, but received weapons, reinforcements, and guidance from North Vietnamese Army soldiers based in the South. The VC fought a guerrilla war of ambush, terrorism, and sabotage, using small units to control villages in the countryside, but leaving the main population centers to government authorities. They were an elusive enemy.

Continued from page 13

February 13, 1965 Americans start Operation Rolling Thunder, a program of air attacks against North Vietnam.

September 18, 1965 1st Brigade, 101st Airborne Division, begins operations in Son Con Valley; the Viet Cong are badly damaged.

October 19, 1965 NVA opens its campaign against the Americans.

November 4, 1965 Battle of the Ia Drang Valley lasts for 35 days; the U.S. 1st Cavalry Division suffers heavy casualties.

November 27, 1965 South Vietnamese army suffers a major defeat in battle at the Michelin Rubber Plantation.

December 15, 1965 First U.S. air raid on North Vietnamese industrial target—a power plant at Uongbi is hit.

U.S. Marines on a search-and-destroy operation against the Viet Cong in June 1965.

September-November South Vietnam
Operation Attleboro sees largest number of enemy dead to date, with 1,106 confirmed casualties.

October

October 24-25 The Philippines
President Johnson and other leaders issue a Declaration of Peace, but North Vietnam ignores the request for a peaceful end to the war.

October 25 South Vietnam
Operation Thayer I begins; it lasts for 111 days.

November

November 30 South Vietnam
Operation Fairfax begins; it will last 380 days and inflict 1,043 casualties on the Viet Cong.

Vo Nguyen Giap

A successful general, Giap was engaged in warfare for most of his long life.

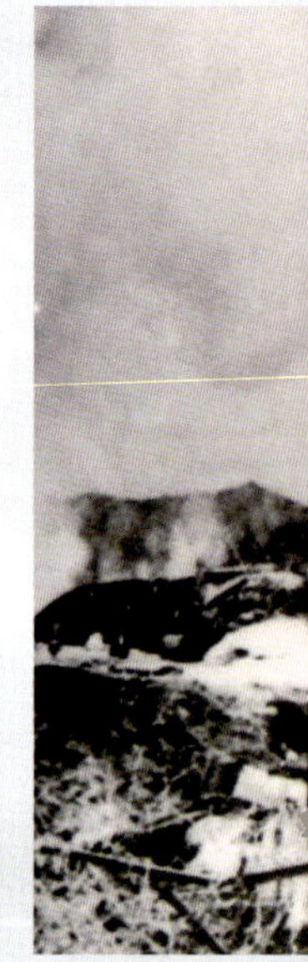

The commander of the forces of North Vietnam, and effectively of the Viet Cong in the South, was Vo Nguyen Giap. Giap had been brought up in a middle-class family in Quang Binh Province, just to the north of the center of Vietnam. His father became involved in nationalist politics and died in prison in 1919. One of his sisters also died after a spell of imprisonment by the French authorities. Giap joined the Communist Party of Vietnam and in 1940 went to China, where he met other exiles, including Ho Chi Minh.

Inspired by Napoleon

In 1942, Giap went back into the northern Vietnamese mountains and began forming guerrilla groups to fight the Japanese who had occupied Vietnam. Giap faced tragedy during this period. His wife and daughter died in prison.

By 1945, Giap had formed a small guerrilla army. He then led military resistance to the returning French colonial authorities. He always claimed that he had been inspired by the examples of Napoleon, but he also used the methods of Mao Zedong, creating a guerrilla army to "swim among the people as the fish swim in the sea."

Giap's genius was in making the countryside unsafe for enemy forces. He won a great victory at Dien Bien Phu in 1954 against the French. In 1968, the siege of Khe Sanh was a failure, however, and the Tet Offensive of the same year led to huge losses for the Viet Cong. Nevertheless, his great moment came when North Vietnamese tanks rolled into Saigon in 1975 and unified the country under communist rule.

KEY DATES

August 25, 1911 Vo Nguyen Giap born in Quang Binh Province, Vietnam.

November 1946 Giap leads fighting against the French colonial authorities in Hanoi and Haiphong. Outgunned, he retreats to the hills.

February 16, 1955 Giap becomes deputy prime minister of newly independent North Vietnam. He builds up Viet Cong forces in South Vietnam over the next eight years.

July 1959 Giap orders the creation of the "Ho Chi Minh Trail." This is a network of routes that keep the Viet Cong in South Vietnam supplied.

1972 Giap launches a failed Easter Offensive against South Vietnam. After this, he takes a lesser role in communist planning.

October 4, 2013 Giap dies in Hanoi.

1 Vo Nguyen Giap devoted his life to the goal of creating a unified, communist Vietnamese state.

2 Giap (left) and Ho Chi Minh in China during the 1940s when they were planning their return to Vietnam.

3 Viet Minh troops carrying a variety of equipment (including a Japanese helmet) during 1946.

4 Viet Minh soldiers raise the communist flag of Vietnam over one of the strongpoints at the French base of Dien Bien Phu.

5 Dien Bien Phu in 1954 was Giap's great victory. Here, French prisoners are led into captivity after their surrender.

An American War

By 1966, the war in Vietnam was "America's War." Soldiers, sailors, marines, and airmen fought the Viet Cong and the North Vietnamese Army (NVA).

→ American troops rest on a bunker. The soldier holds an M79 grenade launcher, often used in jungle firefights.

TIMELINE **1967 JANUARY–DECEMBER**

KEY: Air War | Land War | Politics

January

January 8 South Vietnam
U.S. Army launches Operation Cedar Falls to destroy the enemy around Saigon.

February 21 South Vietnam
Operation Junction City attempts to stop the enemy from fleeing into Cambodia.

March

March 2 South Vietnam
U.S. fighter jets mistakenly bomb Lang Vei village, killing Vietnamese civilians.

March 19 South Vietnam
Viet Cong almost wipe out Fire Support Base Gold, but Americans fight back.

April 24 South Vietnam
A major battle is fought near the Khe Sanh fire base close to North Vietnamese border.

The Viet Cong and North Vietnamese could not match U.S. firepower or maneuverability, but the growing number of U.S. units in Vietnam did not prevent people and material from North Vietnam entering the South via a secret route known as the Ho Chi Minh Trail. U.S. commanders adopted an aggressive search-and-destroy tactic, sending units into hostile territory to seek the enemy. However, the communists usually started the fighting when it suited them and broke off combat when they wanted to, making the search-and-destroy tactic ineffective. With 200,000 North Vietnamese males reaching draft age every year, General Westmoreland's aim of wearing down the enemy could never succeed.

KEY DATES

January 4, 1966 Viet Cong and North Vietnamese Army (NVA) attack a U.S. Special Forces camp using Soviet 120-mm mortars, the heaviest weapon so far used by the North Vietnamese Army.

March 4–8, 1966 Operation Utah sees U.S. Marines and South Vietnamese troops fighting NVA; they lose one-third of troops.

July 7–August 2, 1966 The largest military action of war so far, Operation Hastings, takes place near the DMZ. Over 28 days, U.S. Marines and South Vietnamese troops kill more than 882 Viet Cong.

August 1–25, 1966 Operation Paul Revere in Pleiku Province sees 809 communists killed.

Continued on page 21

UH-1D helicopters airlift troops during Operation Garfield against the Viet Cong, February 17, 1966.

May — August — November — December

May 11 South Vietnam First Battle of Khe Sanh ends with North Vietnamese losses at 940 and U.S. losses at 155.

August 27 South Vietnam The Viet Cong launch raids in the Mekong Delta.

November 2 South Vietnam The Viet Cong launch raids on refugee settlements.

December 8 South Vietnam One of the largest battles in Mekong Delta sees Viet Cong defeated.

Tropical Warfare

"Grunts"—U.S. infantry—had to endure difficult conditions. There were, for example, 131 species of venomous snakes in Vietnam. In the humid climate, minor cuts did not heal and flesh would rot. In the monsoon, soldiers were soaked to the skin, uniforms chaffing their skin. Tins filled with water as they ate. Trails were mined and booby-trapped with concealed pits full of "punji stakes." These sharpened bamboo spears were often smeared with excrement to poison anyone who fell on them.

This map shows how widespread ARVN attacks were in 1966.

U.S. Air Force Operations

As 1966 progressed, the U.S. Air Force's (USAF's) Operation Rolling Thunder increased. It saw sustained bombing of North Vietnam and of hostile targets in South Vietnam and along the Laos border.

The U.S. Navy

The U.S. Navy and its South Vietnamese allies patrolled the many rivers and waterways in southern Vietnam and along the country's long coastline. Operation Market Time (a combined U.S. Navy and South Vietnamese navy effort to stop supplies from North Vietnam) soon began to have an effect on the flow

Soldiers are airlifted by UH-1D helicopters during a search-and-destroy mission.

TIMELINE 1968 JANUARY–DECEMBER

KEY: Air War | Land War | Politics

January

January 30 South Vietnam NVA and Viet Cong launch attacks—the Tet Offensive—across South Vietnam.

January 31 South Vietnam Viet Cong troops hold the U.S. embassy in Saigon for six hours before U.S. troops retake it.

February 23 South Vietnam The siege of Khe Sanh sees heavy shelling by North Vietnamese.

March

March 16 South Vietnam U.S. troops massacre 300 civilians in the small village of My Lai.

May 13 France Peace talks begin in Paris.

A U.S. medical officer treats a villager; such programs aimed to win the trust of the population.

of weapons and fighters reaching the Viet Cong operating in the Mekong Delta in the South.

A Well-Armed Enemy

The year 1966 witnessed a tenfold increase in activity for the U.S. military as it faced a brave and determined enemy. The enemy was also increasingly well armed. American troops found themselves fighting North Vietnamese Army troops equipped with the AK-47 Kalashnikov assault rifle and RP-2s (rocket-propelled grenade launchers).

Throughout 1966, enemy units were employing superior Soviet-supplied weapons. Viet Cong and NVA sappers launched heavy mortar attacks against the Special Forces camp at Khe Sanh and the Da Nang airfield. Soviet 120-mm heavy mortars allowed the communists to launch attacks throughout the South, thereby increasing the problems of base security.

Continued from page 19

August 6–21, 1966 Operation Colorado is a combined U.S. Marine Corps and South Vietnamese operation that kills 674 Viet Cong.

September–November 1966 There are 1,106 communist casualties in Operation Attleboro, the largest number so far killed by U.S. military action.

October 2–24, 1966 Operation Irving is a combined effort of U.S., South Vietnamese, and Korean troops.

October 25, 1966 Operation Thayer I begins.

November 30, 1966 Operation Fairfax starts. It will last for 380 days.

July — October — December

July 1 South Vietnam General Creighton Adams replaces General Westmoreland as commander in Vietnam.

August 23 South Vietnam Communist troops mount their third major offensive this year.

October 31 United States President Johnson announces a complete halt in aerial and naval bombardment of North Vietnam.

November 5 United States Richard M. Nixon elected president by a narrow margin over Hubert Humphrey.

December 29 South Vietnam The United States and South Vietnam will no longer honor holiday truces after the Tet Offensive.

William Westmoreland

From 1964 to 1968, William Westmoreland oversaw a massive increase in U.S. troop numbers in Vietnam.

Westmoreland saw U.S. troop numbers in the country surge to over 500,000 men. He had served in World War II and the Korean War and was thought to be an excellent choice for command in Vietnam.

Westmoreland's first problem was he was fighting an enemy that would not sit still and be defeated by superior U.S. firepower. He had enormous resources in conventional military terms, but the Viet Cong were next to invisible among the Vietnamese villagers and farmers.

Westmoreland's second major problem was the network of trails from North Vietnam through Laos and Cambodia to South Vietnam. These enabled the North to supply guerrillas in the South.

To solve these problems, Westmoreland tried to bring the Viet Cong to battle in large-scale search-and-destroy operations. He used what became a notorious phrase, the "body count," to define success. Identifying who was a Viet Cong fighter was difficult, however, and the figures for dead Viet Cong became inflated.

Khe Sanh

Westmoreland won a final victory when the communists failed to take the base of Khe Sanh during a long siege in spring 1968. However, the simultaneous Tet Offensive against cities and towns meant that the American public saw his strategy as a failure. He left Vietnam in 1968.

KEY DATES

March 26, 1914 William Childs Westmoreland is born in South Carolina.

June 1964 Westmoreland is appointed head of Military Assistance Command, Vietnam (MACV). U.S. military personnel involved in Vietnam number about 16,000 troops.

December 1965 Westmoreland is named *Time* magazine's Man of the Year.

1968 U.S. military personal involved in Vietnam peaks at 535,000.

June 1968 It is announced that Creighton Abrams will replace Westmoreland as head of MACV.

July 18, 2005 Westmoreland dies in South Carolina.

1 General Westmoreland (left) meets President Lyndon B. Johnson who was visiting Vietnam in 1967.

2 Westmoreland (center) and Johnson (right) address the world press outside the White House, defending their strategy in Vietnam.

3 General Creighton Abrams was Westmoreland's successor in Vietnam. He stayed in the post until 1972.

4 Westmoreland took over as Chief of Staff of the entire U.S. Army after his replacement in the Vietnam War.

A Year of Hard Fighting

As 1967 arrived, U.S., South Vietnamese, and Allied forces were locked in a war becoming more intense as more North Vietnamese troops entered the conflict.

↑ The ace of spades on the U.S. helicopter's nose was a deadly omen for Viet Cong troops.

TIMELINE **1969 JANUARY–JUNE**

KEY: Air War | Land War | Politics

January

January 20 United States Richard M. Nixon is inaugurated president of the United States.

February 16 South Vietnam Allied forces observe 24-hour cease-fire during the Tet holiday, but the North Vietnamese break it repeatedly.

February 27–28 South Vietnam Allied forces find huge supplies of enemy arms during Operation Dewey Canyon.

April

April 13 South Vietnam U.S. dead in Vietnam reach 33,641, passing the total lost in the Korean War (1950–1953).

The U.S. and South Vietnamese military carried out ongoing offensives in and along the demilitarized zone (DMZ). Marines in I Corps Tactical Zone started offensives to cut off the infiltration of NVA forces into the Northern and Central Highlands. The leathernecks—the nickname of the U.S. Marines—began setting up the "McNamara Line," a series of electronic sensors and warning systems to warn the Allies of enemy movement in border areas. Despite such measures, Hanoi continued to send soldiers and supplies down the Ho Chi Minh Trail. In the South, Viet Cong activity increased as "Charlie" waged war against Saigon and its U.S. backer. In the Central Highlands, the U.S. Army went on the offensive and inflicted a series of punishing defeats on the enemy.

Navy Actions

The U.S. Navy kept up the pressure on the North Vietnamese and Viet Cong through its

KEY DATES

January 8, 1967 U.S. Army launches Operation Cedar Falls, targeting the Viet Cong in the "Iron Triangle" around Saigon; the U.S. troops seize supplies and destroy enemy positions; many Viet Cong flee.

March 19, 1967 More than 600 Viet Cong die in an attack on Fire Support Base Gold in Operation Junction City.

April 24, 1967 A major battle begins between U.S. Marines and the North Vietnamese Army at Khe Sanh close to the North Vietnamese border.

May 11, 1967 First Battle of Khe Sanh ends with 155 Marines killed and NVA losses of 940.

Continued on page 27

Suspected Viet Cong prisoners await questioning.

May 3 United States
The United States offers to withdraw troops if communists scale back their own attacks.

May 10 South Vietnam
Operation Apache Snow sees heavy losses as U.S. troops try to capture "Hamburger Hill."

May 12 South Vietnam
Viet Cong and NVA launch the largest number of attacks since the Tet Offensive of 1968.

June

June 8 United States
President Nixon announces the first U.S. troop withdrawals in this increasingly unpopular war.

International Allies

America was not alone in fighting. In 1967, President Lyndon B. Johnson's "More Flags" campaign asked allies for support. Among those who sent troops were Australia, Thailand, New Zealand, the Philippines, Taiwan, and Spain. The largest number of non-American troops came from South Korea: 48,000 in 1967. Britain's crack SAS regiment is rumored to have helped. Others sent medical supplies.

The stress of war: a weary U.S. sailor takes a break on board a navy ship.

interception campaign in the Mekong Delta and inland waterways south of Saigon. It also provided backup to air attacks.

Air Strikes on the North

U.S. troops search for the enemy in the network of tunnels where they hid.

The U.S. Air Force maintained steady pressure on the enemy through its three-pronged offensive in the skies over South Vietnam and Laos, and bombing missions against the Ho Chi Minh Trail and petroleum, oil, and lubricants (POL) plants

TIMELINE 1969 JULY–DECEMBER

KEY: Air War | Land War | Politics

July

August South Vietnam
Communist military activity increases throughout Vietnam.

September United States
Racial tensions flare between Black and white Marines.

September 2 North Vietnam
Ho Chi Minh, North Vietnam's president, dies of heart failure.

October

October 15 United States
Vietnam moratorium protests against the war are widely held throughout the United States.

in North Vietnam. It also attacked bridges and major railroads.

Increasing U.S. Troop Levels

On the political front, U.S. president Johnson and his advisors struggled to keep the pressure on North Vietnam. The Johnson administration also tried to placate the highly vocal antiwar movement. But his attempts failed. As the war expanded—over 400,000 U.S. troops would be in Vietnam by 1967—so did the size of the antiwar protests at home. In April 1967, more than 300,000 people demonstrated against the war in New York. Six months later, 50,000 protestors surrounded the Pentagon. Within the United States, support for the war was falling: by the autumn of 1967, only 35 percent of Americans supported the war in Vietnam.

Continued from page 25

August 13–19, 1967 U.S. B-52 bombers carry out raids on different strategic sites in North Vietnam.

August 27, 1967 The Viet Cong attack South Vietnamese civilians in the Mekong Delta.

November 2, 1967 Viet Cong launch a number of raids against refugee settlements, killing civilians and destroying homes.

December 8, 1967 In a large battle in the Mekong Delta, the South Vietnamese 21st Infantry Division trap Viet Cong, who lose 365 soldiers.

December 22, 1967 Korean Marine Brigade begins Operation Flying Dragon.

In the Mekong Delta, the "brown water" navy patrols the waterways.

November 1 South Vietnam
Operation Toan Thang is launched; 5,493 communists will be declared to have died.

November 13–15 United States
A large antiwar demonstration is held in Washington, D.C.

December

December 1 United States
The first drawing of the controversial and unpopular draft lottery takes place.

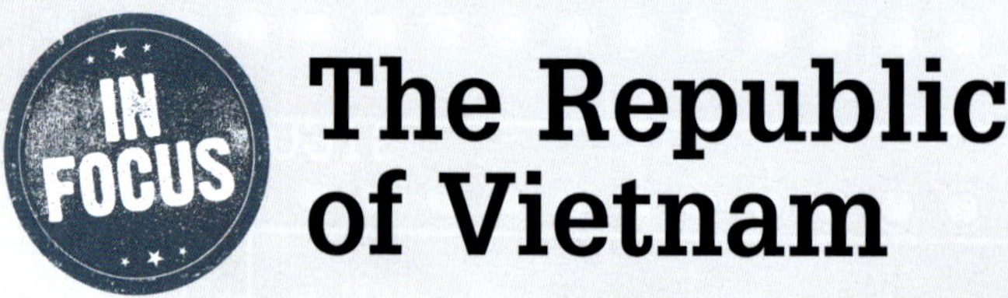

The Republic of Vietnam

The Republic of Vietnam never achieved full legitimacy in the eyes of the Vietnamese people.

A major difficulty facing the U.S. government was the nature of the government of South Vietnam. The U.S. knew who it was fighting against, but what it was fighting for was another question. In the mid-1950s, Ngo Dinh Diem came to power in the South. He had been a nationalist working to end French rule, but his government soon became autocratic and was certainly not democratic. He was a Catholic and promoted Catholics in his administration so alienating Vietnam's Buddhist majority. He even forbade the flying of Buddhist flags at festivals. In 1963 there was the public suicide of Buddhist monks, several of whom burned themselves to death.

Thieu Takes Charge

In November 1963, Diem was overthrown and killed in a coup supported by the U.S. A number of generals jockeyed for his position, but in 1967 General Nguyen Van Thieu became president. He was reelected by a huge majority in 1971, but as he was the only candidate, the election could not be considered democratic. He remained president as U.S. troops and aid were gradually withdrawn from Vietnam. The South Vietnamese Army became weaker until it was overrun in the communist takeover in 1975. Thieu went into exile in the United States.

The lack of a credible South Vietnamese leader who could unite the country was a major reason why many Vietnamese people found the communists more appealing than the alternative.

KEY DATES

1954 Geneva Peace Accords set up two new states, North Vietnam and South Vietnam. The arrangement is intended to be temporary.

June 1955 Ngo Dinh Diem, new leader of South Vietnam, announces he will not participate in elections to unify Vietnam.

1956 Diem launches a land reform program to support Vietnam's people. The plan has stalled by 1960.

January 1959 North Vietnam's politburo (the executive committee for communist parties) approves starting a Viet Cong insurgency in South Vietnam. In 1961, a U.S. intelligence report estimates that substantial portions of the countryside around Saigon are under communist control.

November 1, 1963 Diem is overthrown in a coup. No subsequent government can claim it has a legitimate mandate to rule the country.

1 An ARVN (Army of the Republic of Vietnam) soldier in an M113 armored personnel carrier in the countryside.

2 President Nguyen Van Thieu joins mourners for the people massacred by the Viet Cong in Hué in 1968.

3 ARVN soldiers counterattack against Viet Cong forces during the bitterly fought Tet Offensive of 1968.

4 Ngo Dinh Diem meets President Dwight D. Eisenhower during a visit to the United Nations General Assembly in New York.

Khe Sanh

When its base at Khe Sanh was attacked, the United States responded with heavy firepower, but the commander's strategy later came into question.

U.S. Marines wait to be airlifted during the NVA siege, February 22, 1967.

TIMELINE 1970 JANUARY–JUNE

KEY: Air War | Land War | Politics

January

January 21 South Vietnam
Communist forces attack U.S. troops near the Cambodian border, across which they then retreat.

February 5 France
At the Paris Peace talks, the North Vietnamese produce a letter from a U.S. POW held by the Viet Cong.

February 17 United States
President Nixon announces that the South Vietnamese are taking a larger share in fighting, a process known as Vietnamization.

March 19 Cambodia
Prince Norodom Shanouk, the hereditary monarch of the country, is overthrown.

Khe Sanh was a U.S. forward base constructed around a former French airstrip, close to the demilitarized zone. It was near to the border of Laos, straddling Route 9, which was a major infiltration route used by North Vietnamese troops.

In the summer of 1966, U.S. commander General William Westmoreland strengthened the base at Khe Sanh as a springboard for operations into Laos, which President Lyndon Johnson later vetoed. Through 1967, in particular between April 24 and May 11, troops of the 3rd Marine Division met the North Vietnamese Army (NVA) in a number of fierce pitched battles in the surrounding hills.

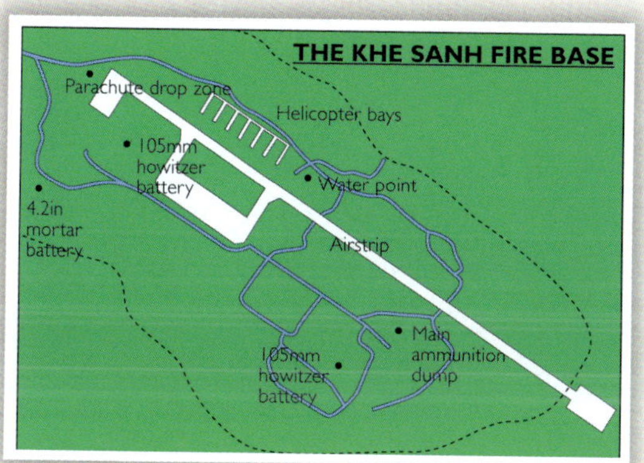

← Khe Sanh guarded the northern provinces of South Vietnam.

KEY DATES

April 24, 1967 Heavy fighting breaks out at Khe Sanh between U.S. Marines and the NVA.

May 11, 1967 The battle ends; the 1st Marine Aircraft Wing has flown more than 1,110 sorties, and U.S. Marine and army artillery units have fired more than 25,000 rounds at the enemy.

January 20, 1968 Fighting around Hill 881 South near Khe Sanh.

January 21, 1968 The NVA begins to shell Khe Sanh and other Marine Corps outposts on hills around the base; the siege lasts 77 days.

↓ Continued on page 33

← Westmoreland aimed to draw the NVA into a set-piece battle at Khe Sanh.

April

June

April 30 United States
There is a public outcry about the attacks into Cambodia.

June 27 Cambodia
The last U.S. and South Vietnamese troops leave Cambodia.

April 29 Cambodia
U.S. and South Vietnamese forces attack North Vietnamese bases in Cambodia.

May 4 United States
Campus protests see four students killed by National Guardsmen at Kent State University, Ohio.

Relief of Khe Sanh

The U.S. Marines initiated an operation to relieve the siege of Khe Sanh on April 1, 1968. Two battalions moved down Route 9 from the east, supported by three brigades of Air Cavalry. Their landing zones came under fire, but an NVA counterattack failed. By April 8, the road was clear. An Air Cavalry trooper hung up a sign at the base proclaiming: "Under new management."

Lessons Learned

In late 1967, U.S. intelligence reports indicated that the enemy was preparing for a major attack. In early January 1968, some 40,000 troops from North Vietnam began converging on Khe Sanh. Westmoreland believed that the enemy intended to grab the northernmost provinces of South Vietnam, prior to opening peace negotiations—just as their forerunners had overrun the French base at Dien Bien Phu in 1954 to help improve their bargaining position at the approaching Geneva Peace Conference. Westmoreland moved 6,000 marines into the area and initiated Operation Niagara, a series of tactical air strikes to break up NVA concentrations. On January 21, the NVA attacked, and the siege of Khe Sanh began.

Devastating Bombardment

U.S. bombers dropped more than 75,000 tons (68,000 tonnes) of high explosives on NVA formations—the largest aerial assault

→ For close fighting, marines used small arms and flamethrowers.

TIMELINE 1970 JULY–DECEMBER

KEY: Air War | Land War | Politics

July

August 30 South Vietnam
Viet Cong attack voters during elections.

October

October 8 South Vietnam
U.S. commanders complete plans to send home a further 40,000 troops by the end of the year.

A U.S. Air Force C-130 Hercules delivers much-needed supplies to Khe Sanh.

on a tactical target in the history of warfare. Around 10,000 communists died at a cost of 500 U.S. Marines. Some NVA units had losses of 90 percent. The NVA's legendary commander, General Giap, almost lost his life when 36 B-52 bombers pounded his field headquarters after U.S. intelligence intercepts revealed that a high-ranking official was in the area.

Westmoreland's Gamble

Khe Sanh was relieved by April 1968, but in June it was abandoned. Westmoreland had taken a huge gamble over a position that was soon dispensed with anyway. His gamble had paid off, but if Khe Sanh had fallen, U.S. involvement in Vietnam would have been ended.

Smoke and dust cover Khe Sanh during a rocket attack.

Continued from page 31

February 23, 1968 NVA artillery gunners and mortars fire more than 1,300 shells in the heaviest shelling of the siege.

April 1, 1968 1st Air Cavalry Division and units from 1st Marines and ARVN begin Operation Pegasus to relieve the beleaguered garrison.

April 15, 1968 Operation Pegasus ends with the relief and resupply of Khe Sanh; casualties stand at 1,011 enemy dead with 51 marines dead and 459 injured.

June 27, 1968 U.S. Marines begin to dismantle the base at Khe Sanh; it is then abandoned.

July 1, 1968 General Creighton Abrams relieves Westmoreland as Commander, U.S. Military Assistance Command, Vietnam.

November 19 North Vietnam
A U.S. raid to free American POWs held in North Vietnam fails as the North Vietnamese move prisoners before the attack.

December

December 3 South Vietnam
The U.S. military presence reaches its lowest total in Vietnam since October 29, 1966, at 349,700 troops.

A Helicopter War

Vietnam is often called the first helicopter war. They had a variety of uses in combat.

In its attempt to fight guerrillas, the U.S. Army made great use of helicopters to transport its troops and to provide close support for the "boots on the ground." The use of helicopters meant that U.S. forces did not need to be thinly spread over the countryside in vulnerable small garrisons. Instead, they could be based in large safe bases and flown swiftly into action. Because the Viet Cong had little or no heavy anti-aircraft weapons U.S. helicopters were at first also relatively safe from being shot down.

1

Helicopter Roles

The workhorse of the U.S. forces in Vietnam was the Bell UH-1 Iroquois. This could transport 13 soldiers into action and machine guns could be fired through its side doors. UH-1 helicopters were first used in Vietnam in 1963. They had three main roles: as slicks (to carry troops into action), as dustoffs (to carry medics and wounded personnel), and as gunships.

As gunships, the UH-1s were not particularly effective, however. They were slow and the design was not suited to absorbing gun recoil. The best attack helicopter of the war was the Bell AH-1 Cobra. This was developed to escort troop-carrying UH-1 helicopters. It was armed with missiles and a forward-facing cannon. Out of nearly 1,110 AH-1s delivered to the U.S. military from 1967 to 1973, 300 were lost during the war.

2

3

4

KEY DATES

1942 Igor Sikorsky's R-4 helicopter goes into production. Some see service in late World War II.

1956 Successful trials of the UH-1 helicopter.

1965 The First Air Cavalry Division arrives in Vietnam. Using its helicopters, it wins an early battle in the la Drang valley, surprising communist forces with their speed and mobile firepower.

1967 First AH-1 attack helicopter is delivered to the U.S. Army.

1968 Helicopter attack groups are developed. They consist of scout helicopters (such as the Hughes OH-6 Cayuse) and attack helicopters (such as the Bell AH-1 Cobra) escorting Bell UH-1 Iroquois troopships.

1 A Ch-47 Chinook delivering supplies. The Chinook could carry loads of up to 7,000 pounds (3,200 kg).

2 UH-1D "Hueys" flying in to evacuate troops in 1966 after one of the big U.S. operations to trap Viet Cong units.

3 An AH-1G Cobra attack helicopter photographed going into action over Vietnam. The Cobra came into service during 1967.

4 A Hughes Cayuse scout helicopter. These were used in combination with UH-1s and Cobras in helicopter attack groups.

Tet Offensive

The Tet Offensive did not give the North Vietnamese the decisive victory they hoped for, but it shattered America's confidence in its ability to prevail in the Vietnam War.

Soldiers of the U.S. 5th Marine Regiment take shelter behind a wall in Hue.

TIMELINE **1971 JANUARY–JUNE**

KEY: Air War | Land War | Politics

January 6 South Vietnam
U.S. secretary of defense Melvin Laird says that Vietnamization is working well; combat missions by U.S. troops will end by the following summer.

January South Vietnam
Enemy activity is apparently in decline. No one can say why.

February 8 Laos
South Vietnamese troops have gone into Laos; no U.S. troops have been sent in at this stage.

April 7 United States
As a further sign that the ground role of U.S. forces is over, President Nixon announces more troop cuts.

January

April

Tet is the Vietnamese Lunar New Year festival. It lasts for seven days and is a time when many Vietnamese travel home to their families. In the first years of the Vietnam War, Tet was marked by a truce. In 1968, that changed.

Caught Unprepared

The Tet Offensive in 1968 took everyone by surprise. There were some signs that a major offensive was on its way, but the U.S. military command expected fighting in the North. President Nguyen Van Thieu was on vacation. Staff at the State Department Vietnam desk in Washington were on leave.

Miscalculation

Until January 1968, most of the fighting had taken place in the countryside. Tet would take it to the cities. City hotels were full of people from the countryside in town for the holiday. In the relatively relaxed atmosphere, it

KEY DATES

January 27, 1968 The supposed seven-day cease-fire for the Tet holiday begins.

January 29, 1968 The Allied cease-fire for Tet begins.

January 30, 1968 In predawn assaults, the North Vietnamese Army (NVA) and Viet Cong launch attacks throughout South Vietnam. This marks the start of the Tet Offensive.

January 31, 1968 Viet Cong troops attack the U.S. Embassy in Saigon and enter the compound. They hold part of it for over six hours. U.S. Marine Corps embassy guards and U.S. Army military police retake the building. They kill all enemy soldiers in the embassy.

February 1, 1968 U.S. forces successfully defend the city of Quang Tri. Operation Hue City to retake the city starts. It will see some of the heaviest fighting of the Vietnam War.

Continued on page 39

Major towns attacked during the Tet Offensive.

April 7–12 South Vietnam U.S. troops launch the five-day Operation Scott Orchard as a demonstration of continuing support for their South Vietnamese ally.

May 3–4 United States Marines are sent to Washington, D.C., to help the police control antiwar protesters.

May 12 South Vietnam Operation Imperial Lake becomes the last major U.S. Marine Corps operation in Vietnam to take place.

June

June 21 South Vietnam U.S. troops continue to leave Vietnam; there are some 244,900 troops that remain in the country.

The Battle for the Citadel

The bitterest battle of Tet and one of the worst atrocities of the war took place around the Citadel in Hue. Communist forces armed with lists of names searched for government officials, doctors, merchants, teachers, clergy, and foreigners. They found and murdered 2,800 people. Some were mutilated, others buried alive in mass graves. Nearly 150 U.S. Marines, 400 South Vietnamese, and 5,000 communists also died.

U.S. marines search for snipers while fighting in Hue.

was easy to infiltrate. On the evening of January 30, 1968, simultaneous attacks began in 100 South Vietnamese cities and towns. The targets included not only the capital, Saigon, but also Da Nang, Hoi An, and Qui Nhon, coastal enclaves thought to be beyond the reach of the communists. The mountain resort of Dalat, previously spared, was stormed.

In most places, the offensive was rapidly put down. But the communists controlled the old imperial capital of Hue for 25 days. More than 4,000 communists in small teams attacked Saigon. A 19-man suicide squad seized the compound

Tanks search for North Vietnamese forces in the Dong Ha area in the aftermath of Tet.

TIMELINE 1971 JULY–DECEMBER

KEY: Air War | Land War | Politics

July

July 9 South Vietnam
U.S. troops are no longer obligated to defend the region south of the DMZ.

July 12 South Vietnam
U.S. troop strength now stands at 236,000; around 14,000 troops are going back home each month.

August 18 South Vietnam
Australia and New Zealand announce the withdrawal of their troops from the war in Southeast Asia.

October 3 South Vietnam
Nguyen Van Thieu's reelection as president is marked by protests and Viet Cong attacks.

of the U.S. Embassy. They held it for 6½ hours, to the horror of Americans watching the battle live on TV.

Televised Brutality

U.S. audiences were shocked to see grinning South Vietnamese soldiers searching bodies for valuables. Many people, including the influential TV anchor Walter Cronkite, concluded that if, after three years of war, the United States could not protect its own embassy, it would never be able to hold the country.

In military terms, the Tet Offensive was a failure. The huge NVA losses (up to 50,000, compared with 2,000 Americans and 4,000 South Vietnamese soldiers) undoubtedly affected their morale. However, the offensive had sent a shockwave through the U.S. military and the public.

Continued from page 37

February 9, 1968 Units of III Marine Amphibious Force beat back 2nd NVA Division's offensive at Da Nang.

February 24, 1968 Marines and ARVN troops finally wrest control of the ancient Citadel in Hue City from the NVA.

February 25, 1968 American forces declare the city of Hue secure, but fighting continues.

February 29, 1968 Extra American troops arrive to prevent defeat in Hue.

March 2, 1968 Operation Hue City ends successfully as the 1st and 5th Marines defeat the NVA assault. Casualties include 142 Marines and 1,943 enemy killed.

The old imperial city of Hue was devastated during the Tet Offensive.

November 12 United States President Nixon declares that U.S. forces now have only a defensive role in Vietnam.

December 31 South Vietnam To date, some 45,626 Americans have been killed during the Vietnam War.

November

December

November 26 North Vietnam As North Vietnam stalls over peace talks, President Nixon authorizes more bombing of North Vietnam.

The War Seen on TV

The Vietnam War has been called the first TV war. Television coverage influenced public opinion at home.

The Vietnam War was the first conflict in which civilians could see the fighting almost as it happened. Technological advances in television meant that journalists could broadcast reports and take cameras onto the battlefield. The result was a series of disturbing stories that stoked opposition to the war back home in the United States.

Key Moments

Some events in particular stood out. The first was the film of the killing of a Viet Cong prisoner by a police chief during the Tet Offensive of 1968. He questioned the man, then drew a pistol and shot him through the head. An NBC crew filmed the incident (albeit without sound), which was also photographed. There were also broadcasts from the compound of the U.S. Embassy in Saigon during the Tet Offensive. Film of dead Viet Cong and of a Viet Cong survivor being led away were a huge contrast to the optimism that U.S. commanders had shown. The footage of the U.S. Embassy almost falling to the enemy and shown on TV shocked the American public.

The U.S. media had supported the war in its early stages, but by the end of the 1960s, most journalists realized there was no victory in sight.

KEY DATES

May 15, 1965 CBS TV hosts a serious debate on the reasons for U.S. involvement in Vietnam.

1965-71 Nightly editions of six o'clock news programs, especially the NBC six o'clock news, feature footage of the fighting in Vietnam.

February 1966 Defense Secretary Robert McNamara gives an off-the-record briefing to journalists in Honolulu. His message: "No amount of bombing can end the war."

February 27, 1968 Respected correspondent Walter Cronkite visits Vietnam soon after the Tet Offensive and writes, "We are mired in stalemate.'"

November 3, 1969 President Richard Nixon tells the American people in a TV address that he will bring U.S. combat troops back from Vietnam.

1971 The *New York Times* reports on documents called "the Pentagon Papers." This is a confidential set of government reports detailing U.S. government involvement in Vietnam from 1945 to 1967. Leaked by Daniel Ellsberg, it shows how the government systematically misled both the public and Congress during the 1960s.

1 The hole that was blasted through the wall of the U.S. Embassy compound in Saigon by Viet Cong during the Tet Offensive.

2 Scenes of violence on television helped to turn the American public against the war as the conflict dragged on.

3 Walter Cronkite prepares to make a broadcast from Vietnam. His pessimism about the war influenced public opinion.

4 Smoke billows across downtown Saigon during the Tet Offensive. This was a sharp corrective to official optimism about the war.

The Death Toll Mounts

The Tet Offensive proved the turning point in the Vietnam War, but there was still more fighting to come. At home, Americans continued to protest against the war.

↑ Helicopters lay a smokescreen during Operation Lamar Plain.

TIMELINE 1972 JANUARY–MAY

KEY: Air War | Land War | Politics

January

January 25 South Vietnam
A new peace initiative is announced by Presidents Nixon and Nguyen Van Thieu to bring the war to an end.

February 21 China
President Nixon becomes the first U.S. president to visit China; he asks for help ending the war.

March

March 10 Cambodia
U.S. ally Lol Non declares himself president of the war-ravaged country.

March 10 South Vietnam
The last American division actively engaged, the U.S. 101st Airborne, leaves Vietnam.

March 23 France
Paris peace talks are suspended as no agreement is reached.

After blunting the Tet Offensive, U.S. forces went after the enemy in an all-out attack, which General Westmoreland hoped would put the enemy on the defensive. Politically, however, 1968 was a period of disengagement for the United States. President Johnson halted the bombing of North Vietnam. The president announced not only that was he willing to discuss peace with North Vietnam's leaders but also that, much to his country's surprise, he would not seek reelection.

Heavy Losses

Although the Tet Offensive had broken the spirit of the Johnson administration, militarily the NVA and VC took heavy losses. The NVA failed to take Khe Sanh or Hue City. For the Viet Cong, Tet was even more damaging. The bulk of its cadres (trained leaders) died in major assaults against Saigon,

KEY DATES

March 16, 1968 U.S. troops massacre more than 300 civilians in My Lai village.

October 31, 1968 President Johnson announces a complete halt in the aerial and naval bombardment of North Vietnam.

November 1, 1968 North Vietnamese officials announce they will meet in Paris with representatives from the United States, South Vietnam, and the Viet Cong to begin peace talks.

November 5, 1968 Richard Nixon is elected U.S. president on a platform of "peace with honor" in Vietnam.

December 29, 1968 United States and South Vietnam announce they will not honor any holiday truces.

Continued on page 45

A tank of A Troop, 3rd Squadron, U.S. 25th Infantry Division, on reconnaissance.

March 30 South Vietnam The North Vietnamese launch major offensive into South Vietnam, known as the Easter Offensive.

April 7 North Vietnam As the Easter Offensive continues, U.S. aircraft resume bombing in North Vietnam.

April 15–20 United States A new wave of protests sweeps university campuses across the United States.

May

May 4 France Peace talks are suspended indefinitely. There is no resolution.

May 8 North Vietnam The U.S. Navy bombs Haiphong and other North Vietnamese harbors to try to cut supplies.

My Lai Massacre

In March 1968, American troops killed 300 people—mostly women and children—in the village of My Lai, South Vietnam. The soldiers also burned the village, angry that some of their comrades had been killed and injured in the area. When the U.S. public learned about My Lai in November 1969, many questioned the conduct of U.S. soldiers in Vietnam. The soldiers' leader, Lieutenant William Calley, was tried and given a life sentence for the killings but was released in 1974.

Hue City, and other U.S. military bases. Despite such losses, North Vietnam nevertheless saw the Tet Offensive and its aftermath as the "beginning of the end" of its quest to unify the country.

The War in 1969

There was still a lot of hard fighting to do in Vietnam. U.S. military strength in South Vietnam peaked at 539,000 men and women before a gradual reduction began. The United States had to train its allies in the Army of the Republic of Vietnam (ARVN) to assume more of the fighting as its own forces began a slow but steady process of redeployment. Despite the announced withdrawal of U.S. forces, the fighting on the ground not only continued, but the tempo of operations

➔ A U.S. howitzer crew fires a shell.

TIMELINE 1972 JULY–DECEMBER

KEY: Air War | Land War | Politics

July

July 13 France
Peace talks resume after a break lasting 10 weeks.

September 16 South Vietnam
With massive support from U.S. aircraft, the South is now defeating the Easter Offensive.

October

October 8 France
A breakthrough at the peace talks when North Vietnam agrees to the continuing existence of South Vietnam.

actually increased. Both sides were eager to position themselves for the approaching fresh peace negotiations, which started again in Paris in early 1969 as a new U.S. president entered the White House.

Determined to achieve "peace with honor," President Richard M. Nixon and his national security advisor, Henry Kissinger, reassured South Vietnamese president Nguyen Van Thieu that the United States would not "cut and run" in its commitment to defend South Vietnam against communist aggression. In private, however, both American politicians sought disengagement from an unpopular war that continued to take hundreds of U.S. lives.

Continued from page 43

February 16, 1969 Allied forces observe 24-hour cease-fire during Tet. Both Viet Cong and NVA forces break the truce at least 203 times.

February 23, 1969 Communist forces launch attacks against U.S. targets across South Vietnam.

May 10, 1969 Operation Apache Snow sees U.S. paratroopers capture the heavily protected Hamburger Hill, named for the amount of blood spilled on it.

September 2, 1969 The president of North Vietnam, Ho Chi Minh, dies.

November 1, 1969 Operation Toan Thang is launched; it results in 5,493 communist deaths.

December 1, 1969 The first drawing of the highly unpopular U.S. draft lottery takes place.

U.S. Marines of the 2nd Battalion, 9th Marine Regiment, relax before operations begin.

November 7 United States Nixon is reelected president of the United States.

November 11 South Vietnam Direct U.S. participation in the Vietnam War ends.

December

December 13 France Talks between U.S. secretary of state Henry Kissinger and North Vietnamese negotiator Le Duc Tho stall again.

December 18 North Vietnam As talks stall, President Nixon orders air attacks against Hanoi and Haiphong.

The Antiwar Movement

From 1965 on, there were protests and demonstrations aimed at stopping U.S. involvement in Vietnam.

American involvement in Vietnam had been questioned back in the 1950s. As a senator, John F. Kennedy believed that the United States should not back the repressive regime of President Diem.

The Draft

In the 1960s, American society was undergoing great changes. The civil rights movement led to changes in the status of Black Americans, but they were disproportionately represented in the casualty lists from Vietnam. Muhammad Ali was stripped of his world heavyweight boxing title in 1966 for refusing to be drafted: "Why should they ask me to put on a uniform and go ten thousand miles from home and drop bombs and bullets on brown people in Vietnam while so-called Negro people in Louisville are treated like dogs and denied simple human rights?" was his comment.

Young people, especially students, opposed the war—some saw it as immoral, some wanted to avoid the draft. Students demonstrated and protested. Four students were killed by National Guardsmen at Kent State University in 1970. In that year, two-thirds of Americans polled said they believed the Vietnam War had been a mistake. They felt it was immoral and a failure of American statesmanship.

KEY DATES

March 1965 Martin Luther King Jr. criticizes U.S. involvement in Vietnam during a speech in Selma, Alabama.

May 5, 1965 Students at Berkeley in California protest the draft and burn draft cards.

October 1967 The editor-in-chief of *Time* writes an article in which he asserts that the war is "not worth winning."

March 16, 1968 Robert Kennedy announces a bid to become the Democratic candidate in the upcoming election, running on an antiwar ticket. He is assassinated in June of that year.

August 26-29, 1968 Riots break out at the Democratic Party Convention as antiwar protesters fight with Chicago police.

1969 News of the My Lai massacre, in which U.S. troops killed hundreds of innocent civilians, reaches the United States.

May 4, 1970 Four protesting Kent State students are shot dead by Ohio National Guard.

1 Antiwar protesters in Wichita, Kansas, in 1967. They questioned the reasons for sending U.S. troops into action in Vietnam.

2 Martin Luther King Jr. spoke powerfully against the war. The civil rights movement became linked to antiwar protests.

3 A student protester offers a flower of peace to military police during a protest at the Pentagon in 1967.

4 Secretary of Defense Robert McNamara, seated left, at a Honolulu conference. He knew the war could not be won.

Operation Rolling Thunder

Begun in March 1965 and continued until November 1968, Operation Rolling Thunder (ORT) was a U.S. and South Vietnamese bombing campaign against North Vietnam.

↑ U.S. Air Force F-105 Thunderchiefs drop bombs on NVA targets in December.

TIMELINE **1973 JANUARY–JUNE**

KEY: Air War | Land War | Politics

January

January 8-12 Paris
Private talks between Kissinger and North Vietnam's Le Duc Tho take place.

January 27 France
The United States, Republic of Vietnam, and Democratic Republic of Vietnam sign a peace agreement in Paris.

January 28 South Vietnam
The final withdrawal of all Allied forces from South Vietnam now begins.

February 21 Laos
A cease-fire is at last agreed.

February 25 Cambodia
Task Force Delta begins secret combat sorties into Cambodia.

An F-4 drops Mk 84 laser-guided bombs over North Vietnam in 1971.

Since the start of the war, U.S. military planners had been eager to bomb North Vietnamese tactical targets such as railroads. However, the administration in Washington, D.C., was concerned about the effect of civilian casualties on public opinion. When the military pressure paid off and Operation Rolling Thunder began, the government had to approve all targets. Bombing was forbidden within 10 miles (16 km) of the capital, Hanoi, for example, in order to protect civilian life

The Campaign Lengthens

Rolling Thunder was intended as a short campaign to demonstrate U.S. air superiority. In 1964, U.S. planners still hoped that it would make North Vietnam abandon its support for communist guerrillas and discuss peace terms. But that initial aim failed, and the bombing campaign was to last for three and a half years.

KEY DATES

August 5, 1964
Johnson orders first air strikes against North Vietnamese targets.

February 13, 1965
Johnson authorizes rolling air attacks on North Vietnamese targets. The first air strikes hit the Ho Chi Minh Trail.

March 1965 U.S. Navy joins Operation Rolling Thunder (ORT); aircraft from carriers USS *Hancock* and USS *Ranger* attack the Phu Qui ammunition depot.

December 15, 1965 U.S. Air Force aircraft destroy a North Vietnamese power plant at Uongbi. This is the first U.S. air raid on a major North Vietnamese industrial target.

Continued on page 51

March

June

June 13 France
The United States, South Vietnam, and North Vietnam sign a starting agreement that puts the Paris Peace Accord into effect; peace seems to have come to Vietnam.

March 27 South Vietnam
This is the last day of the 60-day cease-fire during which some U.S. POWs have been released.

Losing the War at Home

As the 1960s wore on, middle America underwent a shift in its opinion toward Vietnam. At the start, Americans mostly supported military action. By the end of the decade, the majority had turned against it. The Tet Offensive of January 1968 dealt a huge blow to public confidence in America's ability to defeat its enemy. For the first time, it looked as if the United States might not win the war.

As Rolling Thunder went on, the raids grew in size and intensity. U.S. bombers flew missions from bases in Thailand or from aircraft carriers off Vietnam. The missions' aims also changed. The Americans now aimed to demoralize the North Vietnamese civilian population. The United States also wanted to destroy North Vietnam's infrastructure to make it more difficult for the North to send troops and equipment South.

Problems for Pilots

U.S. pilots faced serious problems. Most had been trained for nuclear warfare, not conventional bombing raids. North Vietnam's air defenses had modern ground-to-air artillery from China and the Soviet Union. Its pilots flew slow but highly

➔ Explosions on the ground during Operation Colorado just north of Tam Ky.

TIMELINE **1973 JULY–DECEMBER**

KEY: Air War | Land War | Politics

July

July 1 United States
The new financial year sees U.S. aid to Vietnam massively reduced.

July 30 South Vietnam
Fewer than 250 U.S. military personnel are now in South Vietnam.

August United States
A U.S. district court rules that the secret war in Cambodia is unconstitutional.

August 14 United States
Congress declares the end of U.S.-funded military actions in Southeast Asia.

Phosphorus bombs explode during Operation Georgia.

maneuverable Soviet MiG fighters. By November 1968, an estimated 864,000 tons (784,000 tonnes) of explosives had been dropped on North Vietnam (compared to about 500,000 tons [454,000 tonnes] in the Pacific Theater of World War II). Yet Rolling Thunder had achieved none of its goals. The operation was therefore quietly abandoned.

A flight of B-52 Stratofortress bombers drop their bombs.

Continued from page 49

July 20, 1967 A revised ORT target list is issued. It permits air attacks on 16 additional fixed targets and 23 road, rail, and waterway segments inside the restricted Hanoi-Haiphong area.

August 2, 1967 Hanoi's Paul Doumer rail and highway bridge is hit for the first time. The center span is knocked down and two others are damaged.

August 13-19, 1967 Bridges, bypasses, rail yards, and military storage areas are bombed in an effort to sever communications between Hanoi and Haiphong, the most important deepwater port in the North.

October 25, 1967 Paul Doumer bridge hit again.

December 19, 1967 Rebuilt center span of Paul Doumer bridge knocked out again.

October 31, 1968 Operation Rolling Thunder is halted after failing to achieve its goals.

October United States
In response to the invasion of Cambodia, Congress passes the War Powers Act, limiting the president's power to wage war.

October

December

December 15 South Vietnam
A Joint Military Commission unit is ambushed by a unit of communist troops, and a U.S. soldier is killed.

Cambodia

Cambodia's fortunes fell with the Vietnam War. Its political instability allowed the rise of the Khmer Rouge regime that would devastate the country and its people.

↑ U.S. troops search for Viet Cong bases in Cambodia.

TIMELINE **1974 JANUARY–JUNE**

KEY: Air War | Land War | Politics

February 21 United States
A report claims that the use of defoliants will damage Vietnam for up to a century.

March 22 South Vietnam
The Viet Cong propose a new truce with the United States and South Vietnam.

January — April

April 27–May 2 South Vietnam
The ARVN stages its last major offensive against the North Vietnamese at Svay Rieng.

Like Vietnam and Laos, Cambodia was part of French Indochina. When the French left in 1954, Prince Sihanouk, hereditary ruler of Cambodia, was recognized as the legitimate authority. As trouble brewed in neighboring Vietnam, he courted first the United States, then the North Vietnamese, and then the United States again. North Vietnam, however, used bases over the Cambodian border to provide supplies to its allies in South Vietnam. The supplies were moved southward along the so-called Ho Chi Minh Trail, a network of routes along the Vietnam-Cambodia border.

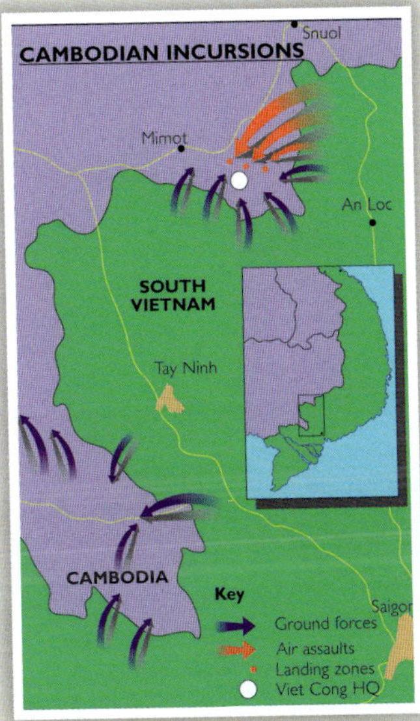

Cambodia Is Bombed

When President Nixon came to power in early 1969, he proposed a secret bombing campaign against Vietnamese strongholds in Cambodia and the Ho Chi Minh Trail. Sihanouk's military supplied the intelligence for the raids, which continued for 14 months. The bombing strayed into inhabited areas, however, and Cambodians died. Casualties rose, and there was unrest.

KEY DATES

1954 French colonial rulers finally leave Cambodia; Prince Norodom Sihanouk is recognized as the country's ruler.

March 19, 1970 General Lon Nol, Sihanouk's prime minister, seizes power in a U.S.-backed bloodless coup.

April 29, 1970 South Vietnamese and U.S. Army forces carry out search-and-destroy operations in a dozen base areas in Cambodia. They are looking to destroy the Ho Chi Minh Trail that allows supplies to be smuggled into South Vietnam by the North Vietnamese. U.S. boats sweep up the Mekong Delta to reopen a supply line to Phnom Penh, the Cambodian capital.

Continued on page 55

The Cambodian incursions in 1970 disrupted communist plans to a limited degree.

May — June

May 9 United States
Congress begins impeachment proceedings against President Richard Nixon.

May 16 South Vietnam
At the Battle of the Iron Triangle, an NVA division takes control of An Dien and continues its advance south.

June
U.S. Marine Anthony Lukeman is designated chief of the Vietnamese Marine Corps.

A Bloodless Coup

In March 1970, Prime Minister Lon Nol staged a bloodless, U.S.-backed coup. In Beijing, Sihanouk set up a government of national unity that included the hard-line communists of the Khmer Rouge. The Khmers' leader, Pol Pot, used North Vietnamese military strength to establish Khmer power on the ground. By 1973, he had built an army of some 40,000 followers.

The Khmer Rouge

When the United States left Vietnam in the 1970s, the NVA pulled out of Cambodia, leaving the Khmer Rouge in control. The Cambodian government fled. On April 17, 1975, the Khmer Rouge entered the capital, Phnom Penh.

Pol Pot believed that, in order to build a perfect communist society, everyone had to become a peasant. He drove people from the cities into the countryside and killed anyone with any

Ho Chi Minh Trail

The trail was a system of mountain and jungle paths and trails used by North Vietnam to infiltrate troops and supplies into South Vietnam, Cambodia, and Laos. It took more than one month's march to travel from North to South Vietnam. By the late 1960s, the trail was wide enough for heavy trucks in places. By 1974, it had some paved roads and underground support facilities, such as hospitals and fuel-storage tanks.

→ U.S. helicopters preparing to leave for a mission into Cambodia, May 14, 1970.

TIMELINE **1974 JULY–DECEMBER**

KEY: Air War | Land War | Politics

July

July 1 United States
U.S. aid to South Vietnam continues to decrease.

August 8 United States
Caught up in the Watergate scandal, President Nixon is forced to resign from office.

August 9 United States
Vice President Gerald R. Ford succeeds Nixon as president.

More U.S. troops and armored vehicles pour into Cambodia.

education or professional skill; even people who wore spectacles were murdered. The result was that little worked. Without trained engineers, dams and irrigation projects built by hand failed. Hundreds of thousands of people who escaped execution starved to death. The Khmer Rouge were thought to be responsible for the deaths of as many as two million of their own people. In 1978, the Vietnamese moved in to stop the killing. The United States had not yet normalized relations with Hanoi, however, so along with many other countries, it condemned the Vietnamese invasion.

Continued from page 53

April 30, 1970 The U.S. and South Vietnamese invasion of Cambodia sparks a public outcry in the United States.

May 4, 1970 As raids into Cambodia continue, U.S. college campuses witness a wave of antiwar protests; at Kent State University in Kent, Ohio, National Guardsmen shoot and kill four student protesters.

June 27, 1970 The last U.S. and South Vietnamese soldiers leave Cambodia; some 4,764 enemy have been killed while U.S. casualties are 399 killed and 1,501 wounded.

April 1, 1975 General Lon Nol flees to the United States.

April 17, 1975 Khmer Rouge, led by Pol Pot, enter Phnom Penh; their hardline communist reign will see two million Cambodians killed in the next three years.

U.S. and South Vietnamese efforts to close the trail failed.

December 13 South Vietnam The North Vietnamese Army begins a new offensive against the South to conquer the country; the NVA is supplied by the Soviet Union.

October

December

December 31 South Vietnam NVA units encircle Phuoc Long City close to the Cambodian border.

The Endgame

As the war grew more unpopular in the United States, U.S. troops were withdrawn from South Vietnam. The war finally ended with a communist victory.

A U.S. AH-1 Cobra gunship in South Vietnam. Its narrow shape allowed it to hide in the trees.

TIMELINE 1975 JANUARY–MARCH

KEY: Air War | Land War | Politics

January

January 7 South Vietnam
The NVA captures Phuoc Long province.

March

March 10 South Vietnam
The NVA attacks Ban Me Thuot at the start of the 1975 Spring Offensive.

March 19 South Vietnam
The South Vietnamese army abandons Quang Tri City and its province.

As the South Vietnamese took on more military duties from the Americans, the U.S. casualty rate fell. Meanwhile, however, the air war continued to inflict casualties on the enemy. By the end of 1970, U.S. and South Vietnamese aircraft had disrupted North Vietnam's ability to launch further Tet-style offensives, but the war was at a stalemate.

Allied Successes

The success of the Allied tactics against communist sanctuaries in Laos and Cambodia, and a campaign against the Ho Chi Minh Trail, forced the North Vietnamese to revert to guerrilla-style tactics. But such tactics, used in the early 1960s, now failed. Efforts by U.S. Marines and the Army of the Republic of Vietnam (ARVN) had helped to turn South Vietnamese peasants against the communists. North Vietnamese Army (NVA) and Viet Cong (VC) attacks on villages increased. Combined U.S. and ARVN pressure ensured the NVA was kept on the defensive throughout 1970.

KEY DATES

February 17, 1970 President Nixon states that the South Vietnamese will take a greater role in fighting, a process known as Vietnamization.

April 29, 1970 South Vietnamese and U.S. forces carry out search-and-destroy operations in Cambodia, prompting a public outcry in the United States.

February 8, 1971 South Vietnamese troops enter Laos.

May 12, 1971 Operation Imperial Lake is the last major U.S. Marine Corps operation in Vietnam.

March 30, 1972 A major North Vietnamese offensive, the Easter Offensive, begins.

Continued on page 59

Private Edward Sellere, U.S. 25th Infantry Division, prepares for a mission.

March 24 South Vietnam Quang Ngai City and Tam Ky fall to advancing NVA; next day, they capture Hue City.

March 26 South Vietnam The NVA captures the former Marine Corps base at Chu Lai.

March 30 South Vietnam The NVA enters Da Nang City and captures the Da Nang Air Base.

The Final Flight

One of the most memorable images of the Vietnam War is the evacuation of people by helicopter from the roof of the U.S. Embassy in Saigon as the city fell to the NVA. The collapse of the South was so quick that plans to evacuate civilians were thrown into disarray. Panic increased as American and Vietnamese fought desperately for a place on the last helicopters to leave Saigon before it fell to the communists.

A Temporary Lull

As the United States turned its attention to ending the war and addressing domestic political problems brought on by the Watergate scandal (1973–1974), Hanoi launched a major offensive during March and April 1972, known as the "Easter Offensive." Supported by U.S. ground advisors and aircraft flying nonstop strikes against waves of North Vietnamese tanks and armored vehicles, the Army of the Republic of Vietnam (ARVN) put up a spirited defense. It later began offensive operations that forced its enemy to seek an armistice. Determined to be reelected and end the war, President Nixon and his national security advisor, Henry Kissinger, used both force and diplomacy in their bid to end the conflict. After a massive bombing campaign against Hanoi during Christmas 1972, the United States introduced an uneasy lull in the war in 1973.

→ When North Vietnam stalled talks at the Paris Peace Talks, Nixon resumed bombings.

TIMELINE **1975 APRIL**

KEY: Air War | Land War | Politics

April

April 17 Cambodia The capital, Phnom Penh, falls to the hardline communist forces of the Khmer Rouge.

April 21 South Vietnam President Nguyen Van Thieu resigns and then flees to Taiwan.

As U.S. forces withdrew, the burden of the fighting fell to the soldiers of the South.

Continued from page 57

April 7, 1972 U.S. bombing of North Vietnam resumes.

December 18, 1972 After peace talks stall again, Nixon orders air attacks against Hanoi and Haiphong.

January 27–28, 1973 Peace agreement finally signed in Paris; the next day, final withdrawal of Allied forces from South Vietnam begins.

December 13, 1974 NVA begins a new offensive against South Vietnam.

April 29, 1975 U.S. Marines evacuate civilians from Saigon.

April 30, 1975 NVA enters Saigon; the conflict is over.

Fall of the South

Between 1971 and 1974, the bulk of U.S. ground and air forces left South Vietnam and turned the war over to the ARVN. The Paris Peace Accords signed in January 1973 seemed to guarantee South Vietnam's survival, but the communists had other ideas. They sensed that victory was close. Each side accused the other of violating the truce. Fighting therefore continued.

With the withdrawal of U.S. forces, the South lacked air support. When the North launched a major offensive in early 1975, the ARVN crumbled and the NVA rolled into Saigon. The Vietnam War had ended in a communist victory.

A memorial stands outside Saigon at the end of the war.

April 28 South Vietnam
General Duong Van "Big" Minh becomes the last president of independent South Vietnam.

April 29 South Vietnam
U.S. Marines carry out Operation Frequent Wind to evacuate Americans and other civilians from Saigon.

April 30 South Vietnam
The NVA enters Saigon and arrests General Minh; South Vietnamese resistance collapses. The long conflict in Vietnam is over.

Aftermath of the War

The Vietnam War had long-term consequences throughout the other countries of Southeast Asia.

The Vietnam War had caused huge human and material damage. Up to three million Vietnamese are thought to have died, along with well over 200,000 Cambodians and perhaps 50,000 Laotians. U.S. deaths in the conflict were 58,220, with 1,626 U.S. personnel listed as missing.

The United States had gone into the war because it feared the spread of communism. However, in the mid-1960s, the seemingly monolithic communist bloc began to crack, and the "Domino Theory" of communism moving from one country to another was seen to be false. In 1965, Chinese and Soviet troops clashed along their common border and from then on, China was clearly outside the orbit of Moscow.

Communist Unrest

After the victory of North Vietnam, it seemed that communism had triumphed in the former French colonies. However, the communist parties of the region soon clashed with each other. Cambodia, renamed Kampuchea, entered a nightmare period of mass killings until it was invaded by Vietnam in 1978. Vietnamese troops remained there until 1989. China, in turn, tried to invade Vietnam in 1979. The communist government in Laos faced insurgency from several political groups.

These wars, sometimes lumped together as the Third Indochina War, contributed to mass emigration, mainly from southern Vietnam. It is estimated that 250,000 refugees died as they fled in small boats from the repressive communist regime.

KEY DATES

January 1975 North Vietnam's army marches into Saigon, soon to be renamed Ho Chi Minh City. Chaotic scenes in the U.S. Embassy as Vietnamese fight to be allowed onto U.S. evacuation helicopters.

April 20, 1975 Communist Pol Pot's Khmer Rouge takes over in Phnom Penh, capital of Cambodia, soon renamed Democratic Kampuchea.

January 1959 Laos becomes a communist state ruled by the Pathet Lao and dependent on the Soviet Union for aid.

January 1959 Pol Pot's regime murders up to 1.8 million Cambodians in an attempt to "purify" the country.

December 1978 Vietnam invades Kampuchea and takes over the country after a short war.

February 15, 1979 China announces an invasion of Vietnam. Its forces withdraw in March of that year.

1 A U.S. soldier on the alert as a helicopter takes off from Saigon during Operation Frequent Wind, the evacuation of 1975.

2 South Vietnamese refugees arrive safely on a U.S. aircraft carrier during Operation Frequent Wind.

3 Vietnamese people in a small, overcrowded vessel flee from the repressive communist regime.

4 Pol Pot, whose followers killed millions of Kampucheans during his quest for a pure form of communism in the former Cambodia.

5 One of the mass graves where Pol Pot's Khmer Rouge buried their victims. It is estimated that the Khmer Rouge murdered between 1.5 and 2 million people.

Glossary

ARVN Army of the Republic of Vietnam (South Vietnam).

cadre A small group of trained people who organize a larger movement.

Charlie U.S. slang for the Viet Cong.

coup d'état A sudden, often violent, seizure of power over a state.

defoliant A chemical used to destroy vegetation that might be used as cover.

delta A low-lying triangular area formed where a river splits into many channels to enter a larger body of water.

DMZ The demilitarized zone, the dividing line between North and South Vietnam established in 1954 by the Geneva Convention.

domino effect A U.S. political theory that if a country became communist, its neighbors were more likely to become communist in turn.

guerrilla A soldier who does not wear uniform and who operates behind enemy lines.

infiltration The penetration of enemy positions without being detected.

intelligence Secret information gathered by espionage.

intercept An intercepted enemy message.

marine A soldier serving on a ship or other naval installation.

NVA North Vietnamese Army.

offensive A coordinated series of military attacks.

sabotage Guerrilla attacks on enemy equipment and infrastructure.

search-and-destroy Describing operations in which troops go into the countryside to hunt for the enemy.

smokescreen A dense cloud of smoke used to hide military maneuvers.

truce A temporary cease-fire.

VC The Viet Cong, the communist guerrillas operating in South Vietnam.

Viet Minh An armed independence movement in Vietnam in the 1950s.

Vietnamization A U.S. policy of handing over fighting to the South Vietnamese.

Further Resources

Books

Atwood, Kathryn J. *Courageous Women of the Vietnam War: Medics, Journalists, Survivors, and More.* Chicago Review Press, 2018.

DeCarlo, Carolyn. *Vietnam War and the Antiwar Movement.* Rosen Publishing, 2020.

DK Eyewitness. *Vietnam War.* Dorling Kindersley, 2017.

Doyle, David. *Vehicles and Heavy Weapons of the Vietnam War.* Pen and Sword Publishing, 2021.

Killcoyne, Hope Lourie. *Key Figures of the Vietnam War.* Rosen Publishing, 2020.

Marcovics, Joyce. *1969 Vietnam War Protest March.* Cherry Lake Publishing, 2021.

O'Connor, Jim. *What Was the Vietnam War?* Penguin Workshop, 2019.

Ward, Geoffrey C., and Ken Burns. *The Vietnam War: An Intimate History.* Vintage, 2020.

Websites

www.vietnampix.com
A pictorial guide to the whole conflict.

www.pbs.org/battlefieldvietnam
PBS site about the battles of Vietnam.

vietnam.vassar.edu
Vassar College overview of the war, including North Vietnamese archive materials.

www.historyplace.com/unitedstates/vietnam
History Place illustrated timeline of the conflict from 1945 to 1975.

www.pbs.org/wgbh/amex/vietnam
PBS American Experience site dedicated to Vietnam Online.

www.vietnamveteransplaza.com/the-vietnam-war/women-in-vietnam/
Women in the Vietnam War.

Index